C000320881

I Love You

Because...

I Love You Because...

A Heartwarmers™ Gift Book

WPL

I Love You Because...

A Heartwarmers™ Gift Book

©WPL 2002

Text by Nick Daws

Illustration by Clare Lake

Printed in China

Published by WPL 2002

ISBN I-904264-10-7

For information on other Heartwarmers™ gift books, gifts and greetings cards, please contact
WPL
14 Victoria Ind. Est. Wales Farm Road
London W3 6UU UK
Tel: +44 (0) 208 993 7268 Fax: +44 (0) 208 993 8041
email: wpl@atlas.co.uk

I Love You
Because...

You may not be perfect,
but you are perfect for me.

You're always there
for me when I need you.

You make me smile
when no-one else can.

With you beside me,
I feel as if I can do anything.

You are the kindest
person I know.

You understand me
better than anyone else.

You say I am the best thing
that has ever happened to you.

I Love You

Because...

You bring out the best in me.

You give me the freedom
to be myself.

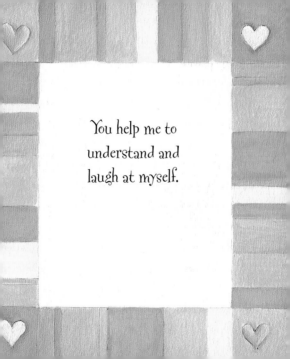

You help me to
understand and
laugh at myself.

You make me feel
good about myself.

I Love You

Because...

You accept me
for who I am.

You don't want
to change me (much)!

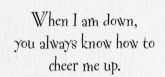

When I am down,
you always know how to
cheer me up.

You are always willing to listen
when I've had a bad day.

You know when
I need a hug.

You always try to
understand my
point of view.

You are never jealous
of my achievements.

You are honest with me,
even when it hurts.

I Love You
Because...

You never make
light of my fears,
however silly they are.

You respect me
and protect me.

You encourage me
to achieve my ambitions.

You've seen me
at my very worst
and you still love me.

You tell me how special I am.

I Love You Because...

You are my soul mate
and my best friend.

You share your
dreams with me.

You confide in me.

You know how to spoil me.

I Love You

Because...

When I'm with you
I don't have to act my age.

We laugh at the
same things.

We can communicate
without even saying a word.

There's nowhere I'd
rather be than by your side.

You give me so much
without even knowing it.

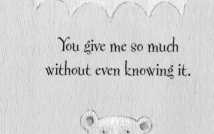

But most of all I love you
because you are YOU !

A Heartwarmers™
Gift Book

WPL